	DATE DUE		

Placed In
The Media Center
In Recognition Of

Judy Keller

For Being A
Very Special
Parent Volunteer
at
Aboite Elementary
School

1996-1997

Read All About Dogs

THE TERRIER BREEDS

Barbara J. Patten

The Rourke Corporation, Inc.
Vero Beach, Florida 32964

PHOTO CREDITS
Photos courtesy of Corel

Library of Congress Cataloging-in-Publication Data

Patten, Barbara J., 1951-
The terrier breeds / by Barbara J. Patten.
p. cm. — (Read all about dogs)
Includes index.
Summary: Illustrations and brief text present various breeds of dogs known as both companions and hunters, including the Cairn terrier, the Dandie Dinmont, and the Airedale terrier.
ISBN 0-86593-458-4
1. Terriers—Juvenile literature. [1. Terriers. 2. Dogs.]
I. Title II. Series: Patten, Barbara J., 1951- Read all about dogs.
SF429.T3P38 1996
636.7'55—dc20 96–23074
CIP
AC

Printed in the USA

TABLE OF CONTENTS

MEET THE TERRIERS

A good day in the life of a terrier might include a little rat-catching, a lot of barking, and some digging in a garden.

These **canines** (KAY nynz), or dogs, take their name from the Latin word “terra” (earth). They have earned their way through history as able hunters and loyal companions. With courage bigger than their bodies, terriers are smart dogs that never quit.

Let’s read about these down-to-earth dogs and find the meaning of “terrier spirit!”

This 12-pound Australian terrier is large courage in a small package.

CAIRN TERRIERS

Wiggling into tight spaces in a rock pile, called a cairn, looking for rabbits or foxes is not easy.

Hundreds of years ago in Scotland, though, it was all in a day's work for the tiny **Cairn terrier** (KAIRN) (TER ee er).

Today Cairns are more likely to be seen rooting in flower beds.

These Cairn terrier pups will never outgrow their love of life.

WEST HIGHLAND WHITE TERRIERS

This Westie is headed home to the castle.

Called "Westie" for short, the baby-faced **West Highland white** (WEST) (HY lund) (WYT) terrier is a serious hunter.

Small in size but big in other ways, the West Highland white terrier is eager to please. Like the Cairn, it seems happy wherever its master may live.

DANDIE DINMONTS

The fuzzy head and short legs on a long, limber body could make you giggle. Add the silly name **Dandie Dinmont** (DAN dee) (DIN mont) and you may have your favorite terrier.

It's hard to think of any dog having a sense of humor, but the Dandie Dinmont seems to. Like clowns, they time their stunts just right to turn a person's frown upside down.

Planning yet another stunt, this Dandie Dinmont is sure to make you smile.

SKYE TERRIERS

A long flowing coat falls over dark brown eyes and covers the body of the Skye terrier . All the hair in the world could not hide this dog's deep sense of devotion to its master.

Like most short-legged terriers, the Skye was first bred for digging rats out of burrows, or holes in the ground.

With its owners, though, this dog is gentle and true. A marker stands in Scotland in honor of a Skye terrier that lived beside its master's grave for 10 years.

The Skye terrier's "veil" of hair once protected its eyes from rats.

BULL AND STAFFORDSHIRE TERRIERS

Sometimes dogs have been abused by humans. Long ago, some breeds were raised for dog fighting. These dogs would fight each other to the death as people cheered. **Bull** (BOOL) and **Staffordshire** (STAF urd SHEER) terriers were two of these canine fighting machines.

Bull terriers are no longer raised for dog fighting.

Today the Staffordshire terrier is a friendly family dog.

Their muscles like steel, powerful jaws, and killer instinct caused these terriers to be feared and honored.

Human kindness over the years has changed these dogs. Today's bull terriers and Staffordshires are living proof that dogs are what people make them.

AIREDALE TERRIERS

Airedales (AIR DAYLZ) are the largest of the terriers, standing about two feet tall and weighing 45 to 50 pounds.

During World War I, these smart, brave dogs carried messages to soldiers in battle. Strong and easy to train, the Airedale also was used in police work.

Today, most Airedales are family pets. They are patient, playful dogs.

"Tucker" is an Airedale terrier that stands 24 inches tall and weighs 60 pounds.

BEDLINGTON TERRIERS

The **Bedlington** (BED ling tun) terrier looks a bit like a lamb, but it acts like a lion. The Bedlington is always ready for action. It is a tough, fast dog.

Bedlingtons were first raised by coal miners to kill rats in the mines. During nightly dog races, their speed was so dazzling that they were nick-named “miner’s racehorse.”

Still a great runner and rat catcher, the Bedlington terrier today makes a good pal and alert watchdog.

A dog pretending to be a lamb describes the Bedlington terrier.

IRISH TERRIERS

Known as "little daredevil," the **Irish terrier** (I rish) (TER ee er) is 25 pounds of courage. Named for Ireland, its homeland, this terrier quickly takes on any enemy, even bigger animals.

At home, though, the Irish terrier is a different story. It is a playful dog that guards its human family.

This Irish terrier shines with "terrier spirit."

SOFT-COATED WHEATEN TERRIERS

Not looking very happy, this soft-coated wheaten terrier may want a hug.

Also from Ireland, the soft-coated wheaten terrier looks more peace-loving than its Irish terrier cousin. A silky wheat-colored coat hides this terrier's zest—but only for a moment.

A fun dog, the soft-coated wheaten has a serious side. It will give its life to save a person.

DOGS IN OUR LIVES

Always on the hunt—for approval as well as prey—terriers have touched human hearts for hundreds of years.

Like all dogs, they need clean water, good food, a warm place to sleep, and medical care to stay happy and healthy.

Owning any dog is a big responsibility. When a dog comes to live with you, it becomes a part of your family. It stays in your family year after year.

If you choose a terrier, those years will pass quickly, with never a dull moment!

The Airedale stands proudly, protecting family and home.

GLOSSARY

Airedale (AIR DAYL) — largest of all terriers, has long legs and wiry tan coat marked with black

Bedlington (BED ling tun) — a breed of terrier from England having a wooly gray or brown coat

Bull terrier (BOOL) (TER ee er) — related to the bulldog. Has a short white coat and pointed snout

Cairn terrier (KAIRN) (TER ee er) — a small dog from Scotland having a wide head and shaggy coat

canine (KAY nyn) — of or about dogs; like a dog

Dandie Dinmont (DAN dee) (DIN mont) — a small terrier with a long body, short legs, droopy ears, and a rough coat

Irish terrier (I rish) (TER ee er) — a breed having a wiry coat of reddish-brown

Staffordshire (STAF urd SHEER) — once used for dog fighting, a big, burly terrier with powerful jaws, wide head, and short hair

West Highland white (WEST) (HY lund) (WYT) — a small terrier from Scotland with upright ears and tail; closely related to Cairn and Skye terriers

Always alert the Australian terrier makes a fine watch dog.

INDEX